The Awesome Book of one-minute MYSTERIES and BRAIN teasers

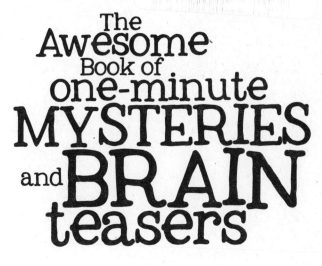

Sandy Silverthorne & John Warner

HARVEST HOUSE PUBLISHERS
EUGENE, OREGON

Cover by Left Coast Design, Portland, Oregom

Cover illustration by Sandy Silverthorne

THE AWESOME BOOK OF ONE-MINUTE MYSTERIES AND BRAIN TEASERS
Copyright © 2009 by Sandy Silverthorne and John Warner
Published by Harvest House Publishers
Eugene, Oregon 97402
www.harvesthousepublishers.com

ISBN 978-0-7369-4973-6 (pbk.)
ISBN 978-0-7369-4974-3 (eBook)

Formerly titled *Return of the One-Minute Mysteries and Brain Teasers*

Printed in the United States of America

15 16 17 18 19 20 21 / BP-SK / 10 9 8 7 6 5 4

To Mr. Walker—thank you for encouraging
my childhood dream of becoming a detective.
And to my wonderful family—Kristin,
Jaxon, and Chloe.

John

To Vicki and Christy—thank you
for all your encouragement, creativity,
and laughter. I love you both.
And to Mrs. Eidam, my high school art teacher,
for encouraging me to stick to the cartooning.
I'm glad I did.

Sandy

Thanks to Jennifer Thomas for "You Get
Nothing for Free." Thanks to Wayne Warner
for "Look What the Cat Dragged In." Thanks
to Kristin Warner for "A Shot in the Dark,"
"Dietary Restrictions," and "Time Will Tell."

Contents

INTRODUCTION

What Are One-Minute Mysteries?

These short mysteries are also known as lateral thinking puzzles, situation puzzles, and yes/no puzzles. Each puzzle describes an unusual scenario, and your job is to figure out what is going on. The puzzles may appear to be open-ended and may seem to have many possible answers, but the goal is to figure out the most satisfying answer, the one that suddenly appears when the lightbulb goes on in your head and you say, "Aha!" (In other words, the solution in the back of the book.) Some solutions may include interesting and possibly unknown facts, but the key to each puzzle can be figured out without any special knowledge. Each mystery takes less than a minute to read, and then you can take your time and enjoy the sleuthing process!

How Do I Solve Them?

The solving process is similar to the game of twenty questions, but you may ask as many questions as you like. You'll need at least one other person to enjoy these puzzles to the fullest, and the more people the better! Choose one person to be the case master, and everyone else is a detective. The case master reads the puzzle aloud and privately consults the solution in the back of the book. The detectives can then pose questions to the case master, who responds by saying yes or no or a phrase like "doesn't matter" or "rephrase your question." If the detectives get stumped, the case master can provide clues as needed.

Solving these puzzles can be a little tricky, so here are a few helpful hints to get you started.

1. Start by asking big-picture questions. You will be tempted to jump right in and guess the answer, but you will most likely be wrong. Instead, start with a broad question so you will have something to build on. As you figure out what is going on, you can ask more specific questions.

2. Always check your assumptions. If a puzzle doesn't come right out and say something, don't assume it is true. Ask yourself, *What am I assuming?* If the case master can't answer one of your questions with a yes or no but instead tells you to rephrase your question, you are probably assuming something that isn't true!

3. The five senses are often important in these puzzles. Ask questions about sight, sound, touch, taste, and smell. Don't forget to check the opposite of what you initially observe. Should the person see, hear, smell, taste, or feel something that he or she can't?

4. Eliminate red herrings. Look at each element of the puzzle and ask if it is important. This way you can focus your questioning on important details.

5. Ask if you are being tricked. Many times these puzzles aren't as straightforward as they seem and are actually leading you to believe something that isn't true.

6. Think laterally. In other words, think creatively or outside the box. If you have exhausted all the obvious possibilities

and don't know where else to go, use your imagination and view the problem from a new perspective.

If you investigate these mysteries on your own, the clues section will serve as your guide. Spend some time really thinking about the puzzle and forming an answer. Does your answer make sense? Is it satisfying? Could another answer work better? Then consult the first clue to see if your answer still makes sense and if you are on the right track. Continue through the clues this way. If suddenly your answer doesn't work anymore, just start over. If you get to the final clue and your answer is still appropriate, check the solution in the back of the book. If all the clues fit with your answer but the solution in the back of the book is different from yours, congratulations—you are clever indeed!

When solving these puzzles, remember to throw out all your assumptions about what is going on. You'll have to think outside the box, use deductive reasoning, and see things from new perspectives. In other words, think like a detective! And one last thing: Don't let the illustrations mislead you. They will generally depict humorous but incorrect assumptions and are purely for your viewing enjoyment.

Now put on your sleuthing caps and get on the case!

Once upon a Crime

1.

Robbed?

Ben tells an officer that his house was robbed the previous night.

"What seems to be missing from your house?" the officer asks.

"As far as I know, nothing." Ben replies.

How does Ben know he was robbed?

2.

For Crime's Sake

A burglar breaks into a stranger's home late at night. He doesn't plan on stealing anything or causing harm, and he isn't seeking refuge. What is going on?

3.

Crime Spree

Two burglars enter a wealthy neighborhood late one night and take everything they can get their hands on. A police officer is upset with what he sees but doesn't do anything about it. Why not?

4.

Caught Red-Handed

A burglar goes out of his way to cover up his hands so he won't leave any fingerprints, but this actually causes him to be convicted for his crime. How come?

5.

Banking on It

A man sat in his car and listened
to a police scanner while his
partner robbed a bank. They
knew the exact whereabouts
of the police, yet they were still
caught. How come?

6.

Shoplifter

Lenny stole some clothes at a store. He forgot to take off the security devices, and when he walked past a scanner, an alarm sounded. But the security guard didn't stop him. Why not?

7.

Unarmed Robbery

Harry hands his receipt to a security guard on duty at the entrance of a store.

"Everything looks fine. The checker must have forgotten to remove a security device again. Don't worry about the alarm. You can go ahead," the guard says as he waves him through.

Yet Harry walks out with a bag full of stolen merchandise. What is going on?

8.

Arrested Development

The police catch Adam in the act of stealing from a store. They don't arrest him, and he isn't sent to jail. He also isn't let off with a warning. What is going on?

9.

Buy the Book

Bud is a petty crook who is always looking for the next scam. He's figured out how to buy new books at illegally low prices. How does he do it?

10.

Going Postal

Jack is a scam artist, petty crook, and all-around sneaky fellow. His latest scheme involves never paying for postage stamps again. Yet Jack continues to send things in the mail, so how does he accomplish this?

11.

Eyewitness

Aaron stops at a red light. Behind him, two masked men with arms full of cash jump into a van and drive off in the opposite direction. Aaron calls 9-1-1 and gives a description of the getaway vehicle. "They're driving a green Volkswagen bus. The license plate is NAVWVYM, and the right taillight is broken." The police never end up apprehending the bank robbers. How come?

12.

Pick a Pocket

Jeffrey watched a man glide
through the crowd, sneaking
things from purses and picking
wallets. This made him very
angry. Jeffrey then deliberately
stood in the thief's path so he too
would be robbed. After Jeffrey
was robbed, he didn't confront
the thief or get the wallet back.
What is going on?

13.

Having a Ball

A burglar waits patiently outside of a house. He can't break into the home until the tenants leave for the day. All he has in his possession is a basketball. How does he plan to break into the house?

14.

Catch Me If You Can

A burglar steals a large sum
of money. The burglary isn't
reported, yet he is arrested
because of his crime. How come?

15.

Letting Down Your Guard

A crooked nighttime security guard steals a
priceless work of art from the museum he
works at. He knows he will get away with it
even though he doesn't frame someone else
for the crime. How come?

16.

At His Fingertips

The scene of a crime was covered with the culprit's fingerprints, but after a detective inspected the prints more closely, he knew that the thief would never be convicted for the crime. How come?

17.

Giving Up Crime

A police officer slams on his brakes when a man
jumps in front of his car, waving frantically for
him to stop. The man tells the officer he is a thief,
so he is promptly arrested. Why did the man turn
himself in?

18.

Locked In and Locked Out

An art thief peeks from his hiding place in the maintenance closet. All is clear now that the museum is closed. He is sure he can avoid the guard, snag his prize, and make it back to his hiding place, but he needs to figure out a way to get back into the closet. The door will automatically lock when he closes it, and he can't prop it open because the guard may notice. He doesn't have a key, so what does the thief do?

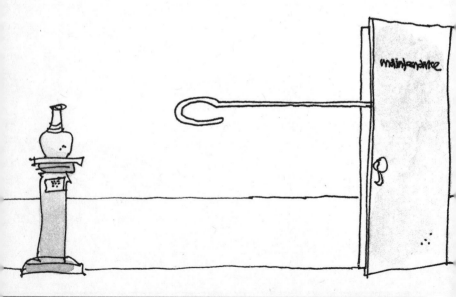

19.

Stolen Car

Ken looks at the shattered glass spread out across the road where his car had been parked the night before. Ken has no idea who took his car or where they took it, but he is pretty sure he will be able to find it. How?

20.

Can't Place a Finger on It

A burglar knew that the police could use prints found at a crime scene to identify a culprit, so he was extremely careful. Actually, he didn't even get a chance to touch anything before he heard a noise come from upstairs. He made a quick escape out the back door, and he didn't leave any prints to connect him to the crime. Why was he arrested for breaking into the home?

SEE THE LIGHT

21.

Lights On, Lights Off

Nathan's mom gets upset when she sees he's left a light on, and lately she's been scolding him even while he uses the light! The problem has nothing to do with Nathan being asleep or awake, so what is going on?

22.

Walk of Courage

Kevin loves taking walks in the park at night. He knows it is risky, but he feels safe with his dog. One evening, his flashlight stops working. He can't see a thing, but he isn't worried at all. How come?

23.

Black Light

Late on a dark night, William drives through an unfamiliar neighborhood. He sees a streetlight go dark and immediately knows that the light didn't burn out. How does he know?

24.

Light Your Way

Mark's flashlight was working
in the darkness, but he still
couldn't see what he was
working on. How come?

25.

A Shot in the Dark

Marsha woke suddenly from her
nap and sat up in her hammock.
She had no idea how long she had
been asleep. Even though she is
completely blind and deaf, she can
still tell it is after dark. It is warm
out, so how does she know?

A PENNY FOR YOUR THOUGHTS

26.

That's a Wrap

John enters a grocery store and notices a woman eating a candy bar in the checkout line. She pays for the empty wrapper without a problem. John eats a snack while shopping, but when he gives the empty wrapper to the checker, she tells him he cannot do that. How come?

27.

Gummed Up

A gumball machine advertises gumballs for 25 cents each. A young boy continues to insert quarters into the machine even though it isn't dispensing any gumballs. What is going on?

28.

You Get Nothing for Free

Jennifer shops around a clothing store and takes her selection to the cashier. "Do you want your receipt with you or in the bag?" asks the cashier. Jennifer takes the receipt and leaves with the bag. When she arrives home, she opens her bag, and it is completely empty. What happened?

29.

Wash Your Troubles Away

The local Scout troop has a car wash
to earn money for summer camp.
A man donates more money than
other customers, but the kids are not
happy. How come?

30.

Paint Me a Picture

A well-known artist sells his works of art for thousands of dollars. Sometimes he chooses to sign his paintings with a pseudonym, even though this makes them completely worthless. Why does he do this?

31.

Hey, Taxi!

Sammy pays a taxi driver $20. He has never ridden in this taxi and doesn't plan to. Sammy wasn't paying someone else's fare and doesn't know the driver. What is going on?

32.

May I Have Your Autograph?

Why does a famous actor's autograph change in value daily?

A Christmas to Forget

Mr. Davis waits until the last minute
to finish his Christmas shopping. Once
he's finished, he takes his gifts for his
nephew to a counter. "That comes to
$67.95," says the woman behind the
counter. Mr. Davis pays and leaves—
without his purchases. How come?

34.

Shortchanged

Bradley doesn't have enough money to pay for his meal, but he pays what he can and is allowed to leave without repercussion. How come?

35.

Money Mirage

Mick wins a bunch of cash during a late-night poker game. The following day he looks for his winnings, but they have disappeared. Mick demands to have his money repaid. The money wasn't stolen, and he didn't misplace it. What is going on?

READ BETWEEN THE LINES

36.

Don't Judge a Book by Its Cover

Richard goes into a bookstore to find a
particular book. He asks a clerk if a copy is
available. After he receives the book, Richard
turns to a certain page, reads a short section,
and then returns the book. He doesn't buy
the book and never will. What is going on?

37.

Food for Thought

Sally keeps a strict diet. She wants to be in the best shape of her life for her wedding day. She records absolutely everything she eats and drinks in her calorie journal. One night, her fiancé points out that she hasn't written down all her calories that day. How is this possible?

38.

Unread Books

Mrs. Carlson has a collection of books she loves. She has owned them for a very long time but has never read any of them even though she is an avid reader. What is going on?

39.

What's the Story?

Kristin begins reading a story that she has never read or heard before, yet she knows what is going to happen. It isn't a true story, so how does she know the ending?

40.

Snail Mail

Matthew didn't receive a response to
his letter for many years. How come?

41.

Nothing to Write Home About

Joel writes a letter, crumples it up, and throws it away. Then he mails a blank piece of paper instead. How come?

42.

Misguided

Alisa's teacher highly recommended a specific guidebook for her trip to Spain over the summer. Alisa buys the correct book, but it ends up being completely worthless. How come?

43.

Cracking the Code

A secret agent used a very common code to encrypt his message, but he knew no one would probably be able to decipher it. How come?

44.

Call Me Sometime

While at a restaurant with her girlfriends, Ashley is approached by a sleazy guy who gives her a piece of paper with his name and phone number on it. "Call me sometime," he says. Later, as she leaves the restaurant, she gives the phone number to the very first person she sees. Why?

45.

Unanswerable

Albert asks his teacher for the answer to one of
the questions on his homework assignment. She
hands him a dictionary and tells him he can find
the answer if he opens to page 167. He opens
the book but can't find anything to do with his
homework assignment on page 167. Why?

THINKING OUTSIDE THE CAGE

46.

Look What the Cat Dragged In

Tim watches his cat carry a mouse to her kittens and drop it in front of them. At first the kittens don't know what to do with the mouse, but soon they begin playing with it. Later, Tim is surprised to find the mouse laying in the yard. Why didn't the cats eat it?

Don't eat now, you'll spoil your dinners.

47.

Do You Noah the Answer?

A boat is filled with many different kinds of animals. They enter in pairs. Predators are right alongside rabbits, horses, and birds, but there is no conflict. What is going on?

48.

In the Doghouse

Ed groans at the sight of his dog squeezing under the fence. Baxter had managed to get into his neighbor's backyard again! Old man Koffer continually threatened to call the pound if Baxter ever set foot on his property again. Luckily for Baxter, Mr. Koffer had left earlier that morning on a summer vacation and wouldn't be back for three months.

Later that year, Ed was confronted by his angry neighbor. "I thought I told you to keep that dog out of my yard!" Ed's dog hadn't been in Mr. Koffer's yard since that first day of Mr. Koffer's trip, so how did the old man know?

49.

Clear as a Bell

Darlene's pet parrot could
imitate the sounds of the
telephone and the doorbell
perfectly. How did Darlene know
when someone was actually on
the phone or at the door?

50.

Birds of a Feather

The climate was the same as in years past, yet some birds flew *north* for the winter. They would usually be living in the south at this time of year. What is going on?

COMMON
SENSES

51.

Nonsense

A condition called synesthesia causes the five senses of hearing, vision, touch, taste, and smell to become mixed up. For example, people may hear colors, see sounds, or taste a touch. In the following situation, Missy may appear to have synesthesia, but can you figure out what is actually going on?

With her eyes closed, Missy was able to smell a color, and she could taste it with just a touch. What color did she smell?

52.

Can You Hear the Music?

Gene listened very intently to the music in his headphones. He didn't like the music, and he knew nothing was hidden in the song, so why was he listening?

53.

How Strange

Lisa looked through her window and saw a stranger walking up her driveway. He rang the doorbell, but before she even had a chance to open her door, the man turned around and walked back down the driveway. How come?

54.

Can You Hear Me?

Jacob saw a woman forming words with her mouth. He couldn't hear her or read her lips, but he knew exactly what she was saying. How?

55.

Will You Fall for It?

Alan works on the top floor of a ten-story building. He looks up from his paperwork and sees a man outside his window. The man is not standing on scaffolding or a platform. What is going on?

56.

Trash Day

Hal sprints toward the garbage. He is extremely
happy when he sees that the garbage truck is late.
Why?

Overdressed

In preparation for their trip to
Hawaii, the Anderson family put on
many layers of clothing. It wasn't
cold in their home town, and it
certainly wouldn't be cold in Hawaii,
so why were they bundling up?

58.

Dietary Restrictions

Even though Carrie is hungry and loves the taste of her meal, she doesn't finish it. She isn't in a hurry and isn't on a diet, so what is going on?

59.

At the End of Your Rope

You look over a cliff and see your pickup a hundred feet below. Your goal is in sight: a cave in the rock face, which is 80 feet down. The treasure is so close! You secure a rope around a tree trunk and lower yourself down the rock wall. When you come to the end of your rope, you are still 20 feet from the cave. You sit on a branch of a tree growing out of the side of the cliff and contemplate your dilemma. How do you make it to the cave?

60.

Banned for All Time

A famous sculptor sold his art for a fortune. The size, subject matter, and quality of his pieces were appropriate for any museum, but he knew he would never see his work displayed in a gallery. How could he be so sure?

TIME OUT
OF MIND

61.

Follow the Leader

Austin embarks on a long journey. He is guided through the morning, but by the end of the day, Austin is leading the way even though he doesn't know where he is going. What happened?

62.

Out of Time

How can you accurately determine when one
hour of time has passed if you don't have a clock,
an hourglass, a sundial, or anything else that is
designed to measure time? Good luck!

63.

At This Point in Time

Will examines a photograph he had taken a few months ago. He notices, for the first time, an analog clock on the wall. Immediately, he knows the clock isn't working and is stuck at a certain time. The clock doesn't appear to be broken, so how does he know?

64.

Late Lately

Allison is waiting at a city bus stop. She is late for school. The schedule says that a bus comes every ten minutes. After waiting for a few minutes, she leaves without getting on a bus. How come?

65.

Crossings

Rob is a deliveryman, and he's in a hurry.
He approaches a railroad crossing as the
barriers start lowering. He won't make it
past before they close, but he doesn't have
time to stop. What does he do?

66.

Late-Night Call

Andy's alarm wakes him up. He rolls over, looks at the clock, and turns off the alarm. "Two in the morning is a horrible time to wake up," Andy groans as he picks up the phone and dials. Why did he make a phone call so early in the morning?

67.

Same Time, Same Place

Bruce's business associate, Dale, was late for their plane trip. Bruce kept his scheduled flight, and Dale took the next flight. The two planes flew at the same speed and took the same amount of time, so the second plane arrived later than the first. Bruce immediately left the airport, taking a taxi to the business conference. Dale did the same when his plane arrived. The two taxis took the same route, had similar traffic, and went the same speed, but Bruce and Dale arrived at the conference at the same time. How is this possible?

68.

Not-So-Fast Food

Jason stood waiting patiently at the local fast-food restaurant for someone to take his order, but even though the restaurant was open and not busy, no one took his order. How come?

69.

Time Will Tell

Carol's clock kept perfect time, but it no longer made any sound. She was sitting across the room and was too far away to see the time, yet she knew exactly what time it was. No other clocks were around. How did she know?

70.

Right of Passage

Koa left his small village and began his journey
to manhood. He was to climb to the tallest peak
and return with a rare flower that only grew from
the highest branches of a 400-year-old tree. Koa
didn't carry a rope or a ladder up the mountain,
and when he finally came upon the tree, he knew
it would be impossible to climb. What did he do?

DRIVING
YOU CRAZY

71.

Free Parking

Alice parks next to an unpaid parking meter. She is late for work and doesn't have any change. She knows this area of town is strictly patrolled and that any vehicle parked illegally will receive a ticket. She walks past the expired parking meter without paying and goes to work. This happens on a normal midweek workday, so why doesn't she receive a ticket?

Speedy like Molasses

Susan drove safely down the freeway going 10 mph under the posted speed limit of 65 mph, yet she received a speeding ticket. How come?

73.

Red Light

Justin drives right through a red traffic light without stopping. A police officer watches him but doesn't do anything about it. Justin isn't driving an emergency vehicle. Why doesn't the cop give him a ticket?

74.

Weather to Travel

Phil and his brother Dave were traveling to
the same destination in different vehicles.
They started at the same place and left at
the same time. Phil's trip was stormy and
overcast, but Dave's trip was clear and
sunny. What is going on?

75.

My Weigh or the Highway

Bob drives his 18-wheeler onto a scale at a weigh station. He is told that he exceeds the weight limit for a bridge on his route. No one removes anything from his truck, but he is permitted to continue on the same route. How come?

76.

Parked Too Fast

Heather speeds past a parked motor-
cycle cop. She is going well over the
speed limit. The officer pulls her over
and gives her a *parking* ticket. How
come?

77.

Alone in the Pool

Peggy receives a ticket for driving in the carpool lane by herself. She knows the officer could see that she didn't have any passengers, but she pleads not guilty. How come?

78.

Park at Your Own Risk

Jay parks his car on the side of the road in a
legal parking spot. When he gets back to his car, a
parking ticket is on his windshield. How come?

79.

Bus Pass

Dana waited patiently for the bus. She was in plain sight, but the bus she was waiting for drove past without stopping. How come?

Tattletale Fine

While driving carefully down the road, Frank was appalled at the other drivers around him. He noticed a parked police officer, so he pulled over to voice his concerns. The officer listened carefully to Frank and then proceeded to write him a ticket! Frank had been driving the speed limit, his car was registered and in perfect working order, and he wasn't intoxicated. What is going on?

81.

Need for Speed

Paul frequently drives on the freeway. He is
perplexed because no one seems to drive the
speed limit. Eventually he figures out what is
going on. Can you?

Good for Nothing

Steve filled out an application for a vanity license plate. He listed his first choice, but he couldn't think of anything for his second choice, so he wrote "nothing" on the form. Unfortunately, a few weeks later, Steve received his brand-new plates with NOTHING printed on them. As it turned out, having NOTHING as a license plate turned out to be quite something! What happened?

83.

Cop Out

Samuel was speeding around a corner when he saw a police officer sitting in his cruiser pointing a radar gun directly at him. Instead of slowing down, Samuel went even faster! The officer turned on his lights and pulled Samuel over and gave him a hefty fine. Samuel wasn't a criminal and wasn't trying to escape, so what was going on?

84.

Sense of Direction

Rod started driving his car west. Without
changing direction or stopping, he was
soon driving east. How?

Parking a Lot

Jeremy waited in a busy parking lot until a spot became available and then parked his car. Instead of going inside the nearby store, he got back into his car and pulled out of his parking spot, which was quickly taken by someone else. Jeremy waited until another spot became available and then parked his car again. He got out of his car again but still didn't go inside. This time he got back into his car and drove off without coming back. What is going on?

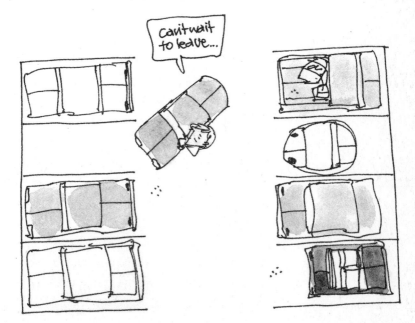

CUNNING
CONUNDRUMS

Stake Her Claim

Amy loves spending her lunch break in the park.
Her favorite spot is on a secluded bench under a
large oak tree. Lately she hasn't been able to get
to the park before someone takes her bench first.
What does she do to claim her spot?

87.

Not from Around Here

The local police find an abandoned
car. The plates are missing, and there
is nothing to identify the car's owner.
With a little detective work, they figure
out that the car isn't from their local
town. How do they know?

88.

In Over His Bread

Mr. Potter gave the following challenge to his students: "Bake a loaf of bread using whatever ingredients you want. The finished product must be edible and must taste like regular bread, but a loaf of bread must be able to support my full weight without collapsing." What did the winning group of students do?

89.

Describing the Unknown

"My friend left her purse here last night. I'm supposed to pick it up for her," Jake told the hostess.

"You'll have to give me a good description of the purse before I can give it to you," she replied.

"But I don't know what it looks like, and I have no way of contacting my friend!" Jake argued.

"Sorry, if you can't prove to me that this is your friend's purse, I can't give it to you. Unfortunately there isn't any identification in here either."

What does Jake do?

90.

Missing Page

Nick and Mike flipped through the tattered phone book they snagged from the phone booth. "Oh man," Nick groaned, "the page we need is missing. It goes from page 119 to page 121!"

But Mike smiled, "I know where the missing page is." Where was it?

PUZZLING
PUZZLES

91.

Giving Thanks

Kent's parents taught him to be very polite and to always say thank you when he is given something. One day he is given something that he likes but doesn't say thank you. What was he given?

Were short on time, please don't thank anyone...

92.

Going the Distance

Tommy hits a baseball so hard that it flies through three states. How is this possible?

Birthday Blues

Benjamin's birthday arrived with no party, no cake, no presents, and no singing. No one even said happy birthday. Benjamin didn't ask people to ignore his birthday. What is going on?

94.

If the Shoe Fits, Don't Wear It

Kenny's favorite shoes still fit him, but he never wears them. They are among many of his other shoes. What is going on?

95.

Sick Day

Gary comes down with a common cold. He feels fine and isn't contagious, but he doesn't go to work. How come?

96.

All Shook Up

Earthquakes happen every single day. Some places are prone to more frequent and larger earthquakes, and other places have fewer and smaller earthquakes. Thousands of earthquakes occur every day around the world, but they are too small to even feel. There is one place where an earthquake has never been charted even though there are seismometers present. (A seismometer is used to measure and record earthquakes.) How is it possible that an earthquake has never occurred there?

97.

Phone Home

Trisha calls home from work and leaves a message on her answering machine. She doesn't live with anyone and isn't leaving a reminder for herself. What is going on?

98.

Locked Door

A door is locked and impenetrable, and Neil doesn't have a key. No one unlocks the door for him, and no damage is done, yet he is able to open the door and enter the house. How?

99.

Locker Up

Brent completely empties out his locker. The next time he opens the locker, something is in it even though he has the only key. How did something get into his locker, and what was it?

Communication Breakdown

Two men who don't know each other are
inhabitants of La Gomera in the Canary Islands.
Their native language is Silbo Gomero, which
is a whistled language. They meet, introduce
themselves, and have a conversation. If they were
from anywhere else, this wouldn't have been so
easy. How come?

Clues

ONCE UPON A CRIME

1. **Robbed?**
   - Something was stolen.
   - No evidence was left behind.
   - Nothing was missing from house.
   - Everything Ben owned was stolen.
   - What kind of house did Ben live in?

2. **For Crime's Sake**
   - The burglar wasn't looking for anything.
   - He has a good reason to be in the house.
   - He is new to burglary, but he isn't practicing.
   - The burglar had been in the house before.
   - He felt very guilty and wanted to make things right.

3. **Crime Spree**
   - The officer isn't restrained and is present.
   - There is nothing the officer can do.
   - The burglars aren't breaking the law.
   - The officer is very jealous of the burglars.
   - A scarecrow, a pirate, and a princess are also envious.

4. **Caught Red-Handed**
   - The burglar didn't have gloves.
   - He covered his hands with something that was convenient.
   - A fingerprinting expert was called in.

- The burglar didn't leave any fingerprints.
- He took off his shoes.

5. **Banking on It**

- The police didn't know the robbers had a scanner.
- The robbers would have gotten away if they hadn't used the scanner.
- The information the man in the car heard on the scanner is irrelevant.
- The robbers were very easy to catch because they made a mistake.
- They couldn't get very far in their getaway car.

6. **Shoplifter**

- The security guard could see the stolen clothes.
- The security guard was present and not distracted.
- Who Lenny is and what kind of clothes he stole are irrelevant.
- The guard knew Lenny hadn't stolen anything from the store.

7. **Unarmed Robbery**

- The checker didn't forget a security device.
- The receipt was Harry's and was completely authentic.
- The guard missed an important detail on the receipt.
- Everything Harry stole was listed on the receipt.
- Harry went to the store twice that day.

8. **Arrested Development**

- Adam is alive, healthy, an adult, and human.
- He really is committing a crime.
- He could have committed any crime without getting arrested.

- He doesn't live in an area without laws and prosecution.
- He still would be penalized.

9. **Buy the Book**
   - Bud doesn't forge coupons.
   - This scam requires going to a store.
   - Bud couldn't do this with all books.
   - This relies on the employee not being observant.
   - Bud doesn't merely switch price tags.

10. **Going Postal**
    - Jack still uses the regular mail and not e-mail.
    - This doesn't involve stealing stamps.
    - Jack abuses the system for returned mail.
    - Mail without postage gets returned to sender.

11. **Eyewitness**
    - The police couldn't find a vehicle matching Aaron's description.
    - Aaron's description wasn't accurate.
    - Aaron was facing forward when he viewed the scene.

12. **Pick a Pocket**
    - Jeffrey wasn't trying to trap the pickpocket.
    - He wasn't upset that a criminal act was taking place.
    - He wants to teach the pickpocket a lesson.
    - The pickpocket didn't steal Jeffrey's wallet.

13. **Having a Ball**
    - Nothing is broken, and timing is crucial.
    - The burglar must act immediately after the tenants leave.
    - He quickly rolls the basketball through a door.

14. Catch Me If You Can

- No one witnessed the robbery.
- The burglar left no evidence behind.
- The burglar was arrested for spending the money.
- The money wasn't marked, didn't have its serial numbers tagged, and wasn't a foreign currency.
- The robbery wasn't reported for a good reason.

15. Letting Down Your Guard

- The guard didn't replace the work of art with a fake.
- He had not planned on stealing the artwork.
- He continues to show up for work after the theft.
- There was a lot of evidence left behind.
- Someone else was accused of the robbery even though the thief didn't frame him.

16. At His Fingertips

- The fingerprints were in perfect condition and weren't faked.
- The fingerprints could be used to connect the thief to the crime.
- The fingerprints weren't ones he was used to seeing.
- The thief would probably spend time behind bars but not in jail.
- People would pay money to come and see the thief behind bars.

17. Giving Up Crime

- The thief wasn't being chased and wasn't afraid of anything.
- The kind of thief the man was is significant.
- The thief didn't want to go to jail.
- He wasn't turning himself in.
- The thief was surprised.

18. **Locked In and Locked Out**

- The thief made it back into the closet.
- The door was closed and didn't look different from either side.
- He didn't pick the lock or break it.
- He kept the lock from engaging.
- He used something that could be found in a maintenance closet.

19. **Stolen Car**

- Ken didn't have any way to track his car.
- He wouldn't need to get the police to help.
- No clues were left behind.
- He would look for the car by himself.
- The car couldn't be very far away.

20. **Can't Place a Finger on It**

- The burglar didn't leave any evidence in the house.
- No one saw him breaking into or leaving the house.
- The burglar wasn't worried about leaving fingerprints.
- He entered through the front door and left through the back door.
- He left something outside the front door.

SEE THE LIGHT

21. **Lights On, Lights Off**

- Sometimes Nathan leaves the light on during the day and sometimes at night, but that doesn't matter.
- Nathan's mom wants to conserve energy but not the energy the light uses.
- Nathan is always hungry but can never decide what to eat.

22. **Walk of Courage**
- Kevin's dog didn't help navigate.
- Kevin had memorized the route.
- He was used to walking in the dark.
- He didn't know the flashlight was burned out.

23. **Black Light**
- William has never been in this neighborhood before.
- The lightbulb wasn't missing and didn't come back on.
- It was a dark and stormy night...

24. **Light Your Way**
- Mark isn't blind.
- He wasn't working on something really small.
- The flashlight was in his possession.
- He didn't need to see something far away.
- He was holding what he was working on, but the flashlight wouldn't light it up.

25. **A Shot in the Dark**
- Marsha couldn't feel anything that told her it was nighttime.
- She was in her own backyard.
- Something happens only after dark.
- She smelled something that told her it was dark out.
- She has a garden.

A PENNY FOR YOUR THOUGHTS

26. **That's a Wrap**
- The wrapper wasn't helpful.
- The checker didn't know how much to charge.

- John ate a healthy snack.
- The wrapper wasn't man-made.

27. **Gummed Up**
- The gumballs weren't really expensive.
- The boy keeps the gumball machine in his room.
- The machine has no gumballs in it.

28. **You Get Nothing for Free**
- Nothing fell out of Jennifer's bag on the trip home.
- Jennifer didn't lose or forget anything.
- Nothing was ever in the bag.
- What did Jennifer buy?

29. **Wash Your Troubles Away**
- The car isn't larger or dirtier than other cars, and it doesn't require more work.
- The kids earned less money during that hour.
- The kids washed fewer cars during that hour.
- The man donated more money because he felt bad.
- He made a mistake that temporarily stopped the fundraiser.

30. **Paint Me a Picture**
- Sometimes the artist wants his identity to be a secret.
- These paintings would actually cost him money if his identity were known.
- These paintings were illegal.

31. **Hey, Taxi!**
- Sammy paid the driver for his taxi service.
- The taxi didn't transport anything for Sammy.
- Sammy has his own car and needs help.

- Sammy isn't very good with directions.

32. **May I Have Your Autograph?**
- Who the actor is doesn't matter.
- The autograph written yesterday doesn't have a different value today.
- The material the autograph is written on is significant.
- The autograph is used to get things.

33. **A Christmas to Forget**
- Mr. Davis isn't planning on coming back, and he didn't forget his gifts.
- The nephew doesn't work at the store where Mr. Davis bought the gifts, and he doesn't have access to the gifts.
- What the gifts are and where Mr. Davis bought them don't matter.
- The presents didn't cost $67.95.
- Mr. Davis wouldn't be seeing his nephew this Christmas.

34. **Shortchanged**
- Bradley didn't come back with more money.
- He didn't have coupons or gift certificates.
- The worker didn't know Bradley paid less than the full amount.
- Bradley paid with change.
- The employee would never know Bradley didn't have enough money.

35. **Money Mirage**
- The money literally disappeared. It was destroyed.
- The money wasn't burned or shredded.
- Mick is to blame for the money being destroyed.
- Mick deserved to have the money refunded.

144   The Awesome Book of One-Minute Mysteries and Brain Teasers

- The money shouldn't have been capable of being destroyed in this method.

READ BETWEEN THE LINES

36. Don't Judge a Book by Its Cover
- The book is very popular.
- You can't buy this book from a bookstore...
- ...even though the store probably has a copy.
- Richard already owned a copy.

37. Food for Thought
- Sally was completely aware of everything she put in her mouth.
- She didn't think about the calories in one item.
- The source of the calories didn't taste very good.

38. Unread Books
- Mrs. Carlson has easy access to the books.
- The books aren't written in a foreign language.
- The books aren't rare, valuable, or in mint condition.

39. What's the Story?
- The story is completely fictional.
- The story isn't told in a movie or on any other recording.
- Kristin knew every single word of the story before she read it.
- This is the only copy of the story in existence.

40. Snail Mail
- The letter took a long time to reach the recipient.
- The response only took a few days to arrive.

- Matthew and the recipient used different mailing methods.
- Matthew didn't know the person who responded.
- Matthew didn't send his letter to a specific person.

41. **Nothing to Write Home About**

- Joel doesn't use invisible ink, and the paper doesn't have a watermark.
- The paper itself isn't important.
- The recipient will do something with the blank piece of paper.
- Something was written on the blank piece of paper.
- The letter Joel threw away and the letter he mailed contained *exactly* the same message.

42. **Misguided**

- The language wasn't a problem.
- The book was about the correct place.
- The author made sure all the information was accurate.
- Although Alisa bought the right book, it was different from the teacher's copy.
- Where she bought the book is important.

43. **Cracking the Code**

- The message wouldn't be destroyed, and it could be intercepted.
- This has nothing to do with computer encryption.
- The language the message is written in is not important.
- If the common code were deciphered, the message still couldn't be read.
- The common code wouldn't be the problem.

44. **Call Me Sometime**

- Ashley didn't give the note to a garbage man or throw it away.

- She figured the person she gave it to needed it more than she did.
- The person was happy but couldn't care less about the phone number.

45. **Unanswerable**
- Albert opened the correct book.
- The teacher wasn't mistaken about where to find the answer.
- Albert didn't have to analyze page 167 to find the answer.
- The answer wasn't in the book anymore.
- The answer was never written in the book.

THINKING OUTSIDE THE CAGE

46. **Look What the Cat Dragged In**
- The kittens were old enough to eat mice.
- The mouse is inedible.
- It wasn't a toy mouse.
- It wasn't an animal.

47. **Do You Noah the Answer?**
- This has nothing to do with Noah's ark.
- The animals aren't caged or confined.
- Every animal is accompanied by at least one person.
- The boat trip is fairly short.
- The animals don't move once on the boat.

48. **In the Doghouse**
- Nothing was broken.
- Mr. Koffer didn't have any surveillance.
- Baxter didn't take anything.
- Baxter left something behind.
- What he left didn't weigh anything.

49. **Clear as a Bell**

- The bird's location and volume don't matter.
- The time of day doesn't matter.
- Darlene could not tell the difference by hearing.
- She can't hear very well anyway.
- Darlene can tell the difference by seeing something other than the parrot.

50. **Birds of a Feather**

- This doesn't usually happen.
- The birds didn't want to fly north.
- These birds don't fly south for the winter.
- This was the first time these birds had ever flown, yet they weren't babies.

COMMON SENSES

51. **Nonsense**

- She literally smelled a color and tasted it with a touch.
- Most people could do this.
- She recognized what it was by its smell.
- She didn't touch it with her hands.

52. **Can You Hear the Music?**

- The music was loud and annoying.
- Gene didn't want to be listening to the music.
- He was alone in a room.
- Gene is a secret agent.
- The headphones weren't plugged into the stereo that was playing the music.

53. **How Strange**

- The man didn't leave anything.

- Lisa didn't have a No Soliciting sign.
- Who the man is and why he was there doesn't matter.
- Lisa wasn't inside her house.

54. **Can You Hear Me?**
- Jacob isn't deaf.
- He wasn't reading what she was saying.
- He didn't know what she was going to say beforehand.
- He couldn't hear her, but he could hear the words she was saying.
- He was driving and listening to the radio.

55. **Will You Fall for It?**
- Alan isn't surprised, and this happens frequently.
- Alan doesn't use stairs or an elevator to get to work.
- Most people don't know the building has ten stories.

56. **Trash Day**
- He doesn't need to throw something in the trash.
- He doesn't need to get something out of the trash.
- He is being chased, and garbage saves his life.
- Luckily for Hal, garbage can be very soft.

57. **Overdressed**
- The Andersons didn't expect to be cold.
- They had packed for every occasion.
- They were following rules.
- They improvised when a problem arose.
- They had room in their luggage for the extra clothes.

58. **Dietary Restrictions**
- Carrie wants to eat more of her meal.

- She has no health-related reason for not finishing her meal.
- She isn't refraining because of present company.
- She doesn't plan on saving the leftovers.
- Carrie wants something even more than the rest of her meal.

59. At the End of Your Rope

- You use your rope.
- You can't make your rope longer or add anything to it.
- You can't climb down to the cave.
- Your pickup is at the bottom of the cliff, so there must be another way down.
- Can you figure out a way to climb up to the cave?

60. Banned for All Time

- People paid for his sculptures but didn't own them.
- A normal museum wouldn't be able to display his work.
- He works in uncomfortable conditions.
- His building materials are very cheap.
- None of his sculptures still exist.

TIME OUT OF MIND

61. Follow the Leader

- Austin's guide wasn't hurt.
- His guide doesn't know where they are going either.
- Austin's journey took him from east to west.
- In the middle of the day, Austin didn't lead or follow.
- Austin journeyed alone, and it was a sunny day.

62. Out of Time

- Do something that takes precisely one hour.
- This can be done while driving on the freeway.
- Think of how we measure how fast we go.

63. At This Point in Time
- The specific time doesn't matter.
- A photo doesn't have to be a static thing.
- Will shouldn't have been able to read the clock.

64. Late Lately
- She has no other way of getting to school.
- She arrives at school and wasn't already there.
- She took a bus to school but didn't get on a bus later.

65. Crossings
- Rob doesn't speed up, slow down, or turn away from the railroad tracks.
- He makes his delivery on time.
- He doesn't drive across the tracks.

66. Late-Night Call
- Andy wasn't calling someone in a different time zone.
- He didn't know the person he was calling.
- He didn't set his alarm to go off at that specific time.
- He got out of bed before he turned off his alarm.
- He didn't have an alarm clock.

67. Same Time, Same Place
- This doesn't involve different time zones.
- Dale was still late to the conference.
- Bruce arrived on time.
- They arrived at the same time of day.

68. Not-So-Fast Food
- No one refused to give him service.
- Jason is a normal human adult.

- The restaurant wasn't too busy.
- Jason wasn't able to get anyone's attention.
- No one knew he was there.

69. **Time Will Tell**

- The clock was analog, not digital.
- Carol knew what time it was because of the clock.
- It was the top of the hour.
- Something alerted Carol of the time.
- She saw something that told her what time it was.

70. **Right of Passage**

- Koa could see the flower growing on the top of the tree.
- The tree was the only thing on the mountain peak.
- None of the flowers had fallen to the ground.
- Koa couldn't have climbed the tree even with a rope or ladder.
- He easily retrieved a flower, but the tree was still standing.

DRIVING YOU CRAZY

71. **Free Parking**

- She parked her vehicle and didn't pay the meter.
- She did nothing illegal and wasn't being clever.
- Other cars received tickets.

72. **Speedy like Molasses**

- The weather and driving conditions are irrelevant.
- Her speed was clocked at 80 mph.
- She got the ticket in the mail.
- Something got between Susan's car and the radar.

73. Red Light

- The officer isn't restrained and is present.
- Justin knows he is driving through a red light.
- Justin isn't doing anything illegal.

74. Weather to Travel

- Dave arrived at his destination sooner.
- The type of vehicle is important.
- The beginning and end of Dave's trip was stormy.

75. My Weigh or the Highway

- Bob crosses the bridge without problem.
- What he is hauling in the truck is irrelevant.
- His truck was barely over the weight limit when it was checked.

76. Parked Too Fast

- The cop gave Heather a warning for speeding.
- The cop had not seen her parked illegally.
- The parking ticket was written an hour earlier.

77. Alone in the Pool

- Peggy was ticketed during carpool lane hours.
- She didn't have any pets in the car.
- No one was hidden in the trunk.
- Peggy had a passenger that couldn't be seen.

78. Park at Your Own Risk

- No parking meter or time limit was involved.
- Jay didn't know he would receive a ticket.
- He got a ticket for parking in a place he shouldn't.
- He was parked for an extended period of time.
- Something changed while he was gone.

79. Bus Pass

- The bus wasn't full or out of service.
- The bus driver could see her waiting at the bus stop.
- Nothing was unusual about Dana, the bus, or the driver.
- Dana eventually got on the bus she wanted.
- The bus turned around but not to pick her up.

80. Tattletale Fine

- The other cars on the road weren't doing anything wrong.
- Frank was elderly and a little confused.
- Frank was doing the exact thing he thought the other cars were doing.

81. Need for Speed

- The freeway isn't crowded.
- This occurs on a stretch of freeway without on/off ramps.
- Paul sees people going slower and faster than the speed limit.
- This occurs when people drive at a constant speed.

82. Good for Nothing

- Steve wasn't happy.
- He wasn't being teased.
- Steve started getting parking tickets.
- The parking tickets weren't his.
- No one else had NOTHING on a vanity plate.

83. Cop Out

- Samuel wasn't in a hurry to get someplace.
- Samuel didn't think he would get a ticket.
- He knew he was speeding and deserved a ticket.
- He usually drove over the speed limit on this road without getting a ticket.

- The police officer who usually was on duty never pulled anyone over.

84. Sense of Direction
- Rod never turned the wheel.
- This didn't involve any stunts or driving upside down.
- Rod's tires never left the pavement.
- The location where this takes place is important.
- He wasn't driving on land, but he was on earth.

85. Parking a Lot
- Neither parking spot was restricted.
- Jeremy could have parked in either spot.
- He didn't have any reason to go into the store.
- Jeremy's car was facing the wrong direction in the first spot.
- He got what he had come for.

CUNNING CONUNDRUMS

86. Stake Her Claim
- Amy doesn't do anything to scare people.
- She leaves a note on her park bench.
- The note doesn't tell people not to sit on the bench.
- Amy's note isn't telling the truth.

87. Not from Around Here
- The car isn't a foreign model.
- The police didn't find any visual clues.
- They found a spare set of car keys.

88. In Over His Bread
- The students had a full kitchen to work in.

- The ingredients were not significant.
- The bread wasn't overcooked.
- The bread was hard as a rock when Mr. Potter stood on it.
- The bread was soft and warm when he ate it.

89. Describing the Unknown

- Jake doesn't give a description of the purse or anything in it.
- He figures out another way to prove he is who he says he is.
- The fact that Jake can't contact his friend is significant.
- Jake does something that a stranger wouldn't be able to do.

90. Missing Page

- Mike didn't see the missing page.
- The boys didn't have to leave the phone booth to find it.
- The page had not been torn out.
- Odd-numbered pages are always on the right.

PUZZLING PUZZLES

91. Giving Thanks

- Kent was happy to receive it.
- It arrived in the mail.
- He knew who gave it to him.
- He was completely comfortable with the person.
- A thank-you was unnecessary.

92. Going the Distance

- This doesn't involve the ball flying over the corners of states.
- The baseball didn't go very far.
- Those states can't be found on a map.

93. Birthday Blues

- Benjamin is alive, healthy, and human.

- Family and friends knew it was his birthday.
- Benjamin didn't care about his birthday.
- His age is important.

94. If the Shoe Fits, Don't Wear It

- They are Kenny's shoes, and he looks at them every day.
- Nothing is wrong with the shoes.
- Kenny is healthy and normal in every way.
- The shoes aren't blocked by anything.
- The shoes are out of reach.

95. Sick Day

- Gary likes his job and wants to go to work.
- He isn't told not to come to work, and spreading germs is not an issue.
- The kind of work Gary does is important.
- Having a stuffed-up nose inhibits Gary's work, but his job doesn't involve smelling things.
- Gary doesn't use his voice and isn't a musician.

96. All Shook Up

- The ground shakes at this spot, but the movement isn't called an earthquake.
- Earthquakes have occurred everywhere in the world to some degree.
- An earthquake will never occur at this spot.
- Why would seismometers be present if an earthquake could never occur?
- Earthquakes happen on earth.

97. Phone Home

- Trisha meant to call home and isn't testing anything.

- No one was in her house, and no one else would be.
- A neighbor had called Trisha at work and complained.
- Something heard her message and responded to it.

98. **Locked Door**

- The door is locked on the inside, and Neil is outside.
- Neil doesn't pick the lock or put anything in the keyhole.
- Someone recently went through the door.

99. **Locker Up**

- The lock wasn't picked, broken, or unlocked.
- This happens to Brent almost every day.
- This isn't the kind of locker you would find in a school or gym.
- The locker can be accessed from the back.

100. **Communication Breakdown**

- It is important that they are whistling.
- Silbo Gomero is the only language that both of them know.
- If English were their native language, they wouldn't be able to communicate.
- There are very few ways these men could communicate.
- Both men are impaired but in different ways.

Solutions

ONCE UPON A CRIME

1. Robbed?

Ben's motor home was stolen along with everything in it.

2. For Crime's Sake

The burglar, after feeling guilty for robbing the house earlier that night, was returning the items he stole.

3. Crime Spree

It is Halloween. The older kids, dressed as burglars, were getting more candy than the younger boy, who was dressed as a police officer.

4. Caught Red-Handed

The burglar used his socks to cover his hands. He didn't realize that toe prints can be just as incriminating as fingerprints!

5. Banking on It

The police scanner drained the getaway car's battery.

6. Shoplifter

Lenny stole the clothes from a different store. When he entered this store, the alarm went off, but the guard waved him through.

7. Unarmed Robbery

Harry actually did buy everything listed on the receipt, but he had done so earlier that day. He then returned to the store and stole every item he had purchased earlier. He now had two of each item and got a steal of a deal—two for the price of one.

8. Arrested Development

Adam is already in jail. He was stealing from the prison canteen.

9. Buy the Book

Bud switches the dustcover of an expensive book with the cover of a cheaper book.

10. Going Postal

Jack switches the destination address with the return address and mails it without postage. The mail will either be "returned to sender," which will go directly where he wants it, or be mailed to him with postage due. If it comes to him with postage due, he asks to have it returned to sender.

11. Eyewitness

Aaron was clearly shaken by the event. He didn't take into consideration that he described the van as he saw it in his rearview mirror. The license plate was actually MYVWVAN (MY VW VAN), and it was the *left* taillight that was broken.

12. Pick a Pocket

Jeffrey was also a pickpocket who was upset that someone else was working in his space. He took the other pickpocket's wallet without him noticing and then made sure the thief would steal his own wallet back. Therefore the man would realize he was being outsmarted and leave.

13. Having a Ball

The burglar rolls the basketball under the closing garage door, triggering the sensor and stopping the door.

14. Catch Me If You Can

The burglar hadn't realized he'd stolen counterfeit money and was arrested for attempting to use it.

15. Letting Down Your Guard

That night, a burglar attempted to steal from the museum, but the guard scared him off. The guard took advantage of the situation, knowing that all the evidence would point to the burglar.

Alternative Solution: That night the museum caught on fire and burned down. The guard took advantage of the situation and stole a painting, knowing that they would think it burned in the fire. *Note: The clues don't work with this alternative answer.*

16. At His Fingertips

The detective could tell that the fingerprints weren't from human hands. Chimpanzee and other primate fingerprints can be distinguished from human fingerprints. (But did you know that koalas' fingerprints are so similar to humans' that even with a microscope, telling the difference is nearly impossible?)

17. Giving Up Crime

When the thief flagged down the undercover police officer and told him he was stealing his car, he wasn't expecting to be arrested.

18. Locked In and Locked Out

The thief put a piece of duct tape over the door latch so it wouldn't lock when he closed the door.

19. Stolen Car

Ken knew his car had been very low on gas and that the thief wouldn't have been able to drive more than a couple blocks.

20. Can't Place a Finger on It

The burglar didn't want to leave footprints in the house so he left his dirty shoes outside the front door. The police later found him sneaking around the neighborhood in his socks, and the dirty shoes were a perfect fit.

SEE THE LIGHT

21. Lights On, Lights Off

Nathan has a habit of leaving the refrigerator door open.

22. Walk of Courage

Kevin is blind. The flashlight was for others to see him.

23. Black Light

Every light on the street went out at the same time, so William knew a power outage had occured.

24. Light Your Way

Mark was trying to adjust the strap on his flashlight, but of course the light couldn't shine back on itself.

25. A Shot in the Dark

Marsha could smell one of her night-flowering plants, which only open up after dark. (Do you know why some flowers open only at night? It is to attract bats and moths, which pollinate only after dark.)

A PENNY FOR YOUR THOUGHTS

26. That's a Wrap

John gave the checker a banana peel. She couldn't charge him without knowing how much the banana weighed.

27. Gummed Up

The boy uses the empty gumball machine as a piggy bank.

28. **You Get Nothing for Free**

Jennifer bought a handbag at the clothing store.

29. **Wash Your Troubles Away**

The man locked his keys in his car. The kids couldn't wash any other cars until he could move it, so they earned less money during that time.

30. **Paint Me a Picture**

The artist doesn't want to go to jail for painting graffiti on walls.

31. **Hey, Taxi!**

Sammy has his own vehicle. He is lost in a new town, so he pays the taxi driver to lead him to his destination.

32. **May I Have Your Autograph?**

The actor writes his autograph or signature on checks.

33. **A Christmas to Forget**

After buying the gifts earlier that day, Mr. Davis went to the post office to mail the presents to his nephew. Overnight shipping can cost quite a bit!

34. **Shortchanged**

Bradley paid with change in the fast-food drive-through. He let the change slip from his hands before the employee was able to take it, and it fell to the ground and under his car. He was allowed to leave so he wouldn't hold up the line. Later, when the employee collected the money, he would assume some of it had rolled away and was lost.

35. **Money Mirage**

Mick accidentally left his cash winnings in his jeans when he put them through the washing machine. When he went to retrieve the money, all that was left was a bunch of disintegrated paper. He immediately knew he had been paid in counterfeit bills because real money won't disintegrate in the washing machine. (Did you know that the reason paper money doesn't disintegrate in the wash is because it is made from cotton or linen fabric?)

READ BETWEEN THE LINES

36. Don't Judge a Book by Its Cover

Richard asked for a phone book so he could find a phone number.

37. Food for Thought

Sally mailed her wedding invitations earlier that day. The glue on each envelope she licked transmitted about ten calories. She invited more than 300 people to her wedding!

38. Unread Books

Mrs. Carlson has a collection of picture books from her childhood, and they don't have any words.

39. What's the Story?

Kristin just finished writing a story, and she is proofreading it for the first time.

40. Snail Mail

Matthew threw a message in a bottle into the ocean. (Did you know that the record for the longest time between sending and finding a message in a bottle is 92 years?)

41. Nothing to Write Home About

Joel is mailing a secret message. The blank piece of paper was underneath the letter he wrote. The recipient will make a pencil rubbing to reveal the impressions of the original letter.

42. Misguided

Alisa made the mistake of buying the guidebook from a used-book store. It was an early edition and was out of date.

43. **Cracking the Code**

The secret agent encrypted his message with a very difficult code. Then he wrote his encoded message in a different code, repeating this process numerous times. The final code he used may have been common and easy to decipher, but he knew that no one would be likely to be able to decipher the more difficult layers of encryption.

44. **Call Me Sometime**

The sleazy guy had written his phone number on a dollar bill. Ashley gave it to a homeless man.

45. **Unanswerable**

When Albert opened the dictionary, the answer key to the homework assignment fell out onto the floor.

THINKING OUTSIDE THE CAGE

46. **Look What the Cat Dragged In**

Tim's cat found a broken computer mouse.

47. **Do You Noah the Answer?**

A ferry boat transports cars and their passengers across a lake. Many cars are named after animals: Ford Mustang, Mercury Cougar, Corvette Stingray, Plymouth Barracuda, Ford Thunderbird, Volkswagen Rabbit, and Jaguar.

48. **In the Doghouse**

Baxter's footprints were perfectly preserved in the concrete Mr. Koffer had poured for his backyard patio the day he left for his vacation.

49. **Clear as a Bell**

Darlene is elderly and hard of hearing, so she has a strobe light that flashes when either the doorbell or telephone rings.

50. **Birds of a Feather**

A group of penguins were flown in an airplane from the South Pole to a zoo in America. (Did you know that penguins don't live in the North Pole? They live almost exclusively in the southern hemisphere.)

COMMON SENSES

51. **Nonsense**

She smelled an orange and touched it with her tongue.

52. **Can You Hear the Music?**

Gene is a secret agent and is listening to a bugging device he had hidden in his target's hotel room. Unfortunately, the target had turned on the radio to full volume, probably knowing that his room was bugged.

53. **How Strange**

Lisa had just pulled her car into her driveway when the man rang her doorbell. He turned around and walked up to her.

54. **Can You Hear Me?**

Jacob was listening to the radio while driving when a woman pulled up beside him. Even though he couldn't hear her, he could tell she was singing along with the same song he was listening to.

55. **Will You Fall for It?**

Alan works in a secret government underground building. The top floor is at ground level.

56. **Trash Day**

Hal is being chased across the roof of a tall building and jumps into a full dumpster.

57. Overdressed

When the Anderson family checked in their luggage at the airport, they exceeded the weight limit. They put on extra clothes to lighten the load.

58. Dietary Restrictions

Carrie wants to save room for dessert!

59. At the End of Your Rope

You tie the end of the rope to the tree you're sitting on. Then you climb back up the rope, untie it from the tree trunk at the top, and let the rope fall down the cliff. You go back down the mountain the way you originally came up, and then you climb up the rope to reach the cave.

60. Banned for All Time

His ice sculptures would melt if they were put on display in a museum.

TIME OUT OF MIND

61. Follow the Leader

Austin started out following his shadow but ended the day leading it.

62. Out of Time

While on the freeway, drive 60 mph for 60 miles. This will take exactly one hour.

63. At This Point in Time

The photograph was taken with a long exposure over a period of a few minutes. If the clock had been working, the second and minute hands would have been blurred. (Did you know that the Hubble Telescope takes a million-second long exposure photograph? That is almost 12 days!)

64. Late Lately

Allison is already on the bus. It stopped to pick up other passengers.

65. Crossings

Rob is driving the train, so he continues through the crossing.

66. Late-Night Call

Andy was awoken by his car alarm. He saw someone breaking into his car and called the police.

67. Same Time, Same Place

Both Bruce and Dale arrived at the conference at eight o'clock. Bruce got there at eight in the morning, and Dale arrived at eight in the evening. Dale's next available flight was 12 hours after the first flight.

68. Not-So-Fast Food

Jason was trying to order food in the drive-through, but he was on his bicycle and wasn't heavy enough to trigger the sensors under the road to alert someone inside.

69. Time Will Tell

Her cuckoo clock didn't make any sound, but when she saw the bird pop out, she knew what time it was.

70. Right of Passage

The tree was a wild bonsai tree and was only a few feet tall.

DRIVING YOU CRAZY

71. Free Parking

Alice is a meter maid.

72. Speedy like Molasses

A swooping bird triggered a speed radar camera that took a

picture of Susan's license plate. She received a speeding ticket in the mail a few days later. (Did you know that the peregrine falcon, the fastest bird on earth, can dive at 217 mph?)

73. Red Light

The police officer is directing traffic in an intersection and motions Justin to drive through.

74. Weather to Travel

Phil drove to his destination while Dave flew in an airplane above the clouds.

75. My Weigh or the Highway

The amount of fuel Bob will use driving to the bridge will put his truck under the weight limit. Diesel weighs seven pounds per gallon, and an 18-wheeler gets about seven miles per gallon. Bob's truck will lose about one pound for every mile he drives.

76. Parked Too Fast

The cop returns a parking ticket that had come loose from Heather's windshield wiper when she drove by.

77. Alone in the Pool

Peggy was pregnant and claimed that her unborn child counted as the second person.

78. Park at Your Own Risk

While Jay was away for an extended period of time, road workers painted the curb next to his car yellow. His legal parking spot became a no-parking zone.

79. Bus Pass

The bus was going the other direction. She knew it would come back soon and continue the direction she needed to go.

80. **Tattletale Fine**

Frank told the police officer that a number of cars were driving the wrong way down the road, when unfortunately it was Frank himself who was driving the wrong way.

81. **Need for Speed**

Paul is driving the speed limit, so he can't see very many cars going the same speed he is. The majority of cars he sees are going either faster or slower than him.

82. **Good for Nothing**

Steve started receiving hundreds of parking tickets in the mail. Apparently, whenever an officer wrote a ticket for a vehicle without a license plate, he wrote "nothing" in the space. The court finally had a place to send all those unpaid parking tickets!

83. **Cop Out**

Samuel knew that the local police had placed a mannequin police officer in a parked police car to act as a speed deterrent. Unfortunately for Samuel, a real police officer was in the car that day!

84. **Sense of Direction**

Rod was driving across an aircraft carrier. During this time, the ship made a U-turn.

85. **Parking a Lot**

Jeremy parked next to a gas pump but then remembered his gas cap was on the other side of the car.

CUNNING CONUNDRUMS

86. **Stake Her Claim**

Amy puts a Wet Paint sign on the bench before she goes to work.

87. **Not from Around Here**

All of the radio station presets transmitted static.

88. **In Over His Bread**

The students froze their loaf of bread until it was completely solid. After the teacher successfully stood on the loaf, they defrosted it in the microwave.

89. **Describing the Unknown**

Jake calls his friend's cell phone, which is still in her purse. He knows her phone number, and his name comes up on her cell phone, so the hostess is satisfied that he is who he says he is.

90. **Missing Page**

Because odd-numbered pages are always on the right and even-numbered pages on the left, the missing pages 120 and 121 can't really be missing because they share the same pieces of paper as pages 119 and 122. Mike instantly realized this and knew that the pages must have been stuck together.

PUZZLING PUZZLES

91. **Giving Thanks**

Kent received a thank-you note in the mail.

92. **Going the Distance**

The baseball flew through three states of matter. It flew through the air (a gas), water from a sprinkler (a liquid), and his parents' living-room window (a solid).

93. **Birthday Blues**

This was the day Benjamin was born.

94. If the Shoe Fits, Don't Wear It

The school bully took Kenny's shoes, tied the laces together, and threw them over a power line.

95. Sick Day

Gary is a taste tester, and because his nose is stuffed up, his ability to taste foods is diminished.

96. All Shook Up

The moon doesn't have *earth*quakes but it does have *moon*quakes. (Astronauts placed seismometers on the moon to record the lunar equivalent of earthquakes. Moonquakes are much less common and weaker than earthquakes, but they have been known to continue for ten minutes!)

97. Phone Home

After Trisha's neighbor called her at work and complained about her barking dog, Trisha called home and told her dog, "Quiet!" over her answering machine.

98. Locked Door

Someone accidentally left a key in the lock.

99. Locker Up

The postal clerk put mail in Brent's post office box.

100. Communication Breakdown

One of the men is blind, and the other is mute. The blind man wouldn't be able to see sign language, and the mute man wouldn't have a way to write in braille. A person who is mute because of problems with his voice box can still whistle by forcing air through his lips. (On a side note, there are people who are blind who can still read sign language by feeling the signs with their hands, but that isn't common.)

Are You Ready for More?

Sandy Silverthorne and John Warner have two more books of one-minute mysteries that will provide hours of fun whether you solve them alone or challenge the sleuthing skills of your friends or family. Challenging enough for adults yet appropriate for detectives of all ages, each puzzle includes a cartoon that adds to the fun.

One Minute Mysteries and Brain Teasers

Mind-Boggling One-Minute Mysteries and Brain Teasers

To learn more about Harvest House books and to read sample chapters, log on to our website:

www.harvesthousepublishers.com

HARVEST HOUSE PUBLISHERS
EUGENE, OREGON